100th Day of School Activities

Written by Hope Blecher-Sass, M.A. Ed.
Illustrated by Howard Chaney
Edited by Jeri Wilcox
Cover Art by Larry Bauer

Table of Contents

Introduction

100th Day of School Activities is a 16-page resource book describing projects teachers can do with their students to celebrate the 100th day of school. Activities include language arts, mathematics, science, art, physical education, community service, and family involvement projects. Learning to count to 100 is an important proficiency in the elementary school curriculum. Using the activities in this book helps to incorporate this aspect of children's education into their daily lives.

Teacher Created Materials, Inc.
6421 Industry Way
Westminster, CA 92683
www.teachercreated.com
©*1999 Teacher Created Materials, Inc.*
Reprinted, 2000
Made in the U.S.A.
ISBN-l-57690-199-8

100 Ways to Celebrate

1. Begin the first day of school by posting the number 1 and updating it daily. This could be an assigned student job.

2. Use the library's Dewey Decimal system to locate 100 books that begin with 100 in the call number or that have 100 in the title.

3. Create math word problems that include 100 in the problem or solution.

4. Read 100 stories with the class, parents, or friends.

5. Begin on the first day of school to keep a people list. Daily, add the name of a person in the class or school. If possible, post a photo or drawing of the person.

6. Shake 100 hands.

7. Hop 100 times; jump rope 100 times; run for 100 seconds; clap 100 times. Organize a fund-raiser for a local charity by getting pledges for your efforts.

8. Collect and send 100 canceled stamps to Stamps for the Wounded, P.O. Box 9176, Silver Springs, Maryland 20916, or Stamps for Children, Harold Effner, Jr., 27 Pine St. Lincroft, New Jersey 07738.

9. Collect postcards and plot their origins on a map. Can you visit 100 places?

10. Read the book *I'll Teach My Dog One Hundred Words* by M. Frith (Random House Books for Young Readers, 1973). Create your own list of 100 words that you can read.

11. Each day, write a sentence that includes the number of the day.

12. Draw a theme-related mural with 100 items on it. For example, the students illustrate 100 living things.

13. Make 100 tube candles and have a make believe party. (See 100th Day Candles activity.)

14. On the first day of school, begin a 100-piece puzzle. Every day a student can add another piece.

15. Choose categories such as cars, people, or foods. Have students cut out 100 magazine pictures and create a collage or story.

16. Use sticky stars or crayons to create your own constellation with 100 stars.

17. Orally count from 1 to 100. Add sign language to your counting recital.

18. Play the game Chutes and Ladders® to learn to recognize the numbers 1–100 and to count.

19. Use the newspaper to keep track of current events. Save one page for each day. On the 100th day, review the events.

20. Use the numbers in the newspaper to make a ruler with 100 centimeters or 100 inches. Use these to measure your height or the length of your hands or feet.

21. Line up 100 people and do a bow or a Rockettes-style kick.

22. Take or collect 100 photos of your students and create an oral or written story about them.

23. Collect 100 used greeting cards and use them to create graphs, tally charts, or word problems for each other to solve. Also, look for patterns, learn sight vocabulary, and attach a blank piece of paper to create a new card.

24. Create a large hundreds-chart bulletin board. Students can use it to demonstrate addition, subtraction, skip counting, inequalities, etc. This can be used as an interactive bulletin board.

25. Collect 100 used books. During parent-teacher conferences, have a book sale with each book priced between $.25 and $1.00.

26. Invite people to the class or school to have a 100 book read-a-thon.

27. Read the book *One Hundred Hungry Ants* by Elinor J. Pinczes and use it to learn about math, patterns, and ants. (See Ants activity.)

28. Read *The One Hundred Dresses* by Eleana Estes (Harcout Brace, 1974) and then design 100 dresses on paper. For career awareness, invite a dress designer and share some of your creations.

29. With the assistance of parents, keep track of the students who pledge not to watch TV for 100 hours. Reward those who succeed.

30. Between 5 P.M. and 10 P.M., begin with one class to create a rhyme for the number one. Pass it on to the next class who creates a rhyme for the number two. Continue to 100. Submit it to a local newspaper for publication.

31. Make hats decorated with 100 items. Wear them to school on the 100th day.

32. Use straws and string to create a snake with 100 ways to wiggle. Follow up with a discussion of vertebrae movements and snakes. (See Ways to Wiggle activity.)

33. Estimate which combination of students' weights will equal 100 pounds or kilograms. Use a scale to weigh people and confirm estimations.

34. Stack, balance, and compare sizes of 100 blocks or 100 boxes.

35. Do a connect-the-dots puzzle with the numbers 1 to 100. Create and share your own connect-the-dots puzzle.

36. Find and classify 100 food pictures. You can also use the photos to create menus.

37. Find advertised items in the newspaper and add them to total $100.

38. Study probability by flipping a coin 100 times and charting the heads versus the tails outcomes.

39. Count 100 kernels of unpopped popcorn. Discuss how the heat will change it. Weigh and compare the volume of the popcorn before and after it is popped. Share the popcorn.

40. Walk 100 paces. See how far you have gone. Measure the distance for comparison to feet and yards.

41. Trace 100 hands or feet.

42. Create a mosaic with 100 paper squares.

43. Read *The Wolf's Chicken Stew* by K. Kasza (Putnam Publishing Group, 1987) and then bake 100 pancakes, donuts, or cupcakes. Contact a local farmer or veterinarian to visit and learn about animal diets, hens, and chicks. Use this for lessons on counting, estimation, measurement, classification, graphing, animal diets, and food groups.

44. Give someone 100 hugs.

45. Look at something that is 100 years old, such as a camera, and compare and contrast it to its modern version.

46. Brainstorm with friends a list of 100 toys, 100 movies, or 100 books. Graph the items by likes, the ease with which they are played or read, etc.

47. Use a deck of cards and play Go Fish. See who can collect 100 points.

48. Have a spelling bee with 100 words.

49. Learn about nutrition and health by reading labels and identifying foods with 100 calories. This can also incorporate physical activity by doing exercises that will burn 100 calories.

50. Create a weight-bearing structure using only 100 toothpicks and glue or tape. Put weights on it to see how much it can hold.

51. Go bowling and see who can score 100 points.

52. Read *Winnie the Pooh* books, emphasizing the 100 Acre Wood setting. Create your own 100 Acre Wood map, story, characters or puppets.

53. Read *Curious George Rides a Bike* (Houghton Mifflin, 1973) and make 100 newspaper boats to float. Discuss floating versus sinking and bicycle safety.

54. Cut a plastic milk bottle across the diameter to make a large cup. Fill the bottle with water. Insert a small floating Styrofoam plate. One at a time, add paper clips, pieces of chalk, buttons, or small manipulatives onto the plate. Predict how many you can add before it will sink. Compare the results

to the actual number. Can you make 100 paper clips float? The tops of the milk jugs can be used as sand scoops or shovels. (See Floating Pennies activity.)

55. Collect 100 newspapers, cans, etc., to recycle.

56. Measure 10 lengths of string in multiples of 10 units. Display them for comparisons to real objects or pictures of real objects that correspond to the heights.

57. Contact a local hospital and make Happy 100th-Day-of-School-cards to send to babies born on that day.

58. Write the alphabet and try to create 100 words from the 26 letters.

59. Write your telephone numbers, including the area code. Add the numbers. Does any sum equal 100?

60. Contact a local 4-H club or forestry service and find out if there is a tree 100 years old located in your area. Visit it and learn about tree growth rings. (See Tree Rings activity.)

61. Use a computer, a dictionary, or another resource to find real words with 5 letters, 10 letters, 15 letters, 20 letters, 25 letters, 50 letters, and possibly 100 letters. If you can't find them, invent a word and its meaning and submit it as a guest editorial to a local newspaper or dictionary publisher.

62. Count your pulse rate for 100 seconds, or monitor how long it takes your heart to beat 100 times.

63. Research fossils that are 100 years old. Make modeling clay fossils or use small chicken bones, shells, ferns, and leaves set in plaster of Paris to create your own fossil keepsake.

64. Use magnifying glasses and/or microscopes to look at items enlarged up to 100 times. Orally and through illustrations, compare and contrast the details.

65. When hockey season begins, choose a team to follow and estimate when they will reach a total of 100 goals. Chart their games and scores on a graph.

66. Learn about community helpers and careers by listing words and pictures of 100 different jobs.

67. Learn about buildings that are 100 stories high. Through illustrations, blocks, Lego®, or Lincoln Logs®, create your own building and then explain what it would be used for.

68. Watch the movie *Fantasia*. Record 100 different musical selections. As you listen, illustrate what the music makes you think of. Compile a class musical impressions book.

69. Create a construction paper chain which is 100 inches (cm) or 100 feet (m) long. Decorate the classroom with paper chains. Incorporate a pattern such as AB or ABC into it for added interest.

70. Collect 100 caps and create a class version of the book *Caps for Sale* by Esphyr Slobodkina (Scholastic, Inc., 1993). Invite local nursing home residents or daycare center participants to come to a reading of the story. Afterwards, distribute the caps to the audience.

71. Collect 100 apples and cook them to make applesauce. Estimate how many people you can feed and how much the applesauce will weigh. Then invite your parents to eat it. You can also use 100 peanuts to make peanut butter.

72. Make a giant hopscotch game using the numbers 1 to 100 and play the game with other students.

73. Have a basketball shooting contest to score 100 points or see who can make the most baskets out of 100 tries.

74. Use liquid bubbles and blow 100 bubbles. Observe how many stay for the duration of the activity.

75. Collect 100 used videos or books and then donate them to local nursing homes.

76. Using your phone numbers, look at the numbers as a sequence to find the number 1, then 2, 3 . . . all the way through 100.

77. Using Roman numerals write the numbers 1 to 100 and make a list of places where you observe these numbers.

78. Create a geometric figure with 100 sides and name it.

79. On the 100th day of school, pool and graph the attendance rates of students to observe who has 100% attendance. The teacher or principal can distribute a certificate or special prize to the students with 100% attendance.

80. With the assistance of peers, teachers, and parents, learn to count from 1 to 100 in another language, possibly learning to write it, too.

81. Use the numbers 1 to 100 to play Bingo.

82. During the first day of school, plant a few seeds and photograph the class. Weekly, chart the plants' growth. On the 100th day, photograph the plants and students and then compare and contrast the plants' growth to those of the students.

83. Make 100th Day of School buttons.

84. Use index cards to construct your own set of dominoes. Either create a set with up to 100 dots or, as each pair plays, have them add their scores to determine when the winners reach 100 points.

85. On a chart, list the numbers 1 to 100. Each day, write what one student ate for lunch. By the 100th day, did the group eat 100 different lunches?

86. Collect 100 *TV Guides*. Use each to create paper trees. Decorate for a centerpiece or donate to a local shelter or nursing home. (See TV Trees activity.)

87. Each day have a person add one piece of Lego® or a block to a class creation. What do you have by the 100th day?

88. Create a time capsule. Bury it and leave a marker. At the local library, leave a notice about the location with instructions that it be opened in 100 years.

89. Using the number words one to one hundred, create your own word search or crossword puzzle.

90. Get to know your state by compiling a list of 100 places families can visit. Submit your list to the state tourism board for potential publication.

91. Slice apples into 100 circles and collect the seeds. Use the seeds for comparisons and collections. String the circles and then dip them into diluted lemon juice. Hang the apples to dry. The apple strings can be used as decorations or for art activities. (See Apple Strings activity.)

92. After Halloween, bring in and weigh your collection of treats. Did anyone collect 100 ounces? Ask each person to donate a few treats to give to a local pediatric center or family shelter.

93. Obtain a set of magnetic words. Can you create 100 different sentences?

94. Collect 100 buttons and socks. Create different patterns and make puppets. Entertain each other, create story characters, or give the puppets to others.

95. Collect 100 used, but clean, neckties. Use labels to number each tie. On a bulletin board arrange them in a right-and left-side cascade to create an evergreen tree. Afterwards, donate the ties to a shelter.

96. Learn about space travel. If you were traveling to the moon for 100 days, what would you pack?

97. Create 100 nesting dolls. Use these to tell stories, give as gifts, or to share. (See Nesting Dolls activity.)

98. Connect 100 jumbo paper clips. Use this length as the standard unit to measure classroom dimensions, students' heights, etc.

99. Using fingerpaints, have the children make 100 hand prints. Either arrange the prints to make specific pictures or create a collage. Use magnifying glasses to examine the differences in prints.

100. Using unlined 3" x 5" (8 cm x 13 cm) memo pads with 50 or 100 sheets, have the students animate one or two characters. Flip through the pages to watch the characters move. Invite an animator to visit the class. Use the flip book to produce a 100th day movie or cartoon. (See Animation activity.)

100th Day Candles

Celebrate the 100th Day with make-believe candles you create yourself. Send home the note below requesting toilet-paper tubes. Assemble the completed candles into a cake pan or box lid, decorated as a cake. Take a picture of your students and their 100th Day "cake" which can be used in your school yearbook.

Materials:

- 100 empty toilet-paper tubes
- glue or tape
- scissors

- red and yellow construction paper, cut into 2" x 3" (5 cm x 8 cm) rectangles
- pencils, crayons, or paint
- 10 large, shallow rectangular boxes

Directions:

Divide the class into 10 groups of students. Each group will make a birthday cake. Color or paint the tubes. Draw and cut the red and yellow construction paper into flame shapes. Make the red flames a little larger than the yellow flames. Glue the smaller yellow flames onto the red flames. Glue the red flames to the inside of the tubes. Write students' names and the date on the candles. To commemorate the 100th Day of School, have each group glue 10 candles on top of a box decorated like a birthday cake.

Have a wonderful party!

Dear Parents/Guardians,

We will be needing empty cardboard toilet-paper tubes for a 100th Day art project. Please have your child bring_____ tubes to class by_____. Thank you for your help with this project.

Sincerely,

_____

© *Teacher Created Materials, Inc.*

Ants

Get parents actively involved in their children's education with this literature- and math-related lesson based on the book, *One Hundred Hungry Ants* by Elinor J. Pinczes (Houghton Mifflin, 1994). Pick a sunny day when everyone can have fun marching around the schoolyard!

Materials:

- 100 plastic or paper ants
- 100 students or a combination of students and parents
- index cards numbered 1 to 100 which can be taped onto participants

Directions:

Read and discuss the book. Have the students practice walking in two rows, in four rows, and in five rows. If you can, gather 100 people and have them count off into two groups of 50 and then walk in rows. Follow this with a regrouping into four sections of 25 people who then march in rows; follow with five groups of 20 and 10 groups of 10. If the groups are getting confused with the count, you might want to label the individuals with their respective numbers.

For a classroom activity, count the 100 plastic ants or cut your own ants from the pattern on this page. Use these to replicate the patterns in the book and to demonstrate division and addition.

> **Ant facts:** Ants have been on the earth for at least 100 million years and are found almost everywhere. The ant has three major body parts: the head, which contains the eyes, brain, mouth, and two antennae; the thorax, which contains the digestive tract and the six legs; the abdomen, which contains the stomach, anal gland, and stinger. There are also some ants that have wings attached to the thorax section. Ants usually live in nests or cavities in the soil, wood, or leaves. Their diets range from arthropod eggs to indiscriminate items such as bread crumbs.

Ant Patterns

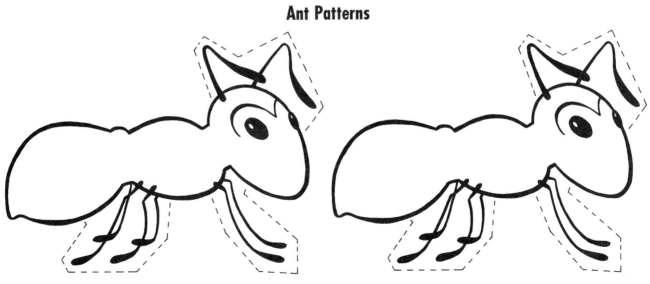

Ways to Wiggle

This project is an excellent cooperative group activity which will assist students in understanding how vertebrae affect the movements of snakes as well as humans. First, students can be asked to imitate the movement of a snake. The teacher can then show them a snake skeleton and a human skeleton or pictures of each. Students can locate their own spines and feel the motion as they bend and flex. Finished snakes can be named and placed in a center for further experimentation and measuring applications. The length of the snakes can be compared to the heights of the students or other objects.

Making a Straw Snake

Materials:

- scissors
- string
- plastic straws
- construction paper or cardboard
- white glue

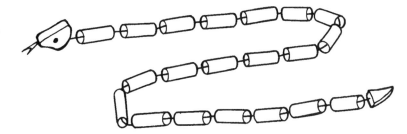

Directions:

To make the straw snake, cut a piece of string 4.9 feet (1.5 meters) long. Dip the end into glue and allow it to dry so it is stiff enough to thread through the straws. Cut 100, one-centimeter long pieces of straw. Knot the unglued end of the string through one of the straw pieces so the remaining straws will not slip off. Continue threading the straw pieces onto the string. Allow enough space between pieces so the straw pieces (vertebrae) will be flexible. Leave enough string on the end to knot the last piece of straw. Cut a head and tail out of construction paper or cardboard and glue them onto the string. Ask students to touch the snake and bend it. Have the snake crawl over the edge of a desk or book and slither around a pencil or cup. What do they observe about the snake's ability to wiggle? As an alternative, have groups make snakes with different-sized pieces. Use the form below to compare and contrast the movements. Can your snake move in 100 different ways? How long is a snake with 100 vertebrae? One member of each group will give a report on their findings to the class.

- -

Ways to Wiggle

Date_____ Group Name_____

Members_____

Name of snake _____

Number of vertebrae_____ Length of each vertebra_____

Length of snake _____

Ways to wiggle which we discovered (demonstrate or draw pictures)

_____

_____

Floating Pennies

For this experiment you will need to collect at least 100 pennies. If you are conducting it as a cooperative group exercise, you will need 100 pennies per group. Send home the note below requesting Styrofoam plates. (You may wish to substitute Styrofoam with aluminum foil made into boat shapes.)

Materials:

- a deep clear container
- Styrofoam plates
- water
- pennies

Directions:

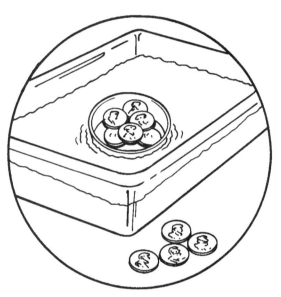

Fill the clear container $1/3$ to $1/2$ full with water. Carefully place the shallow plate onto the water. Demonstrate that the plate is to remain floating. Give each student a penny and, one by one, have the students place their pennies onto the plate. Before each penny is added, the group should predict whether the plate will continue to float or if it will sink. After several have been placed on the plate, have students predict how many pennies they think the plate will hold before it sinks. Predictions can be recorded on a chart. After placing the pennies, compare the prediction with the actual result.

Questions for Discussion:

Can 100 pennies be put on the plate before it sinks?_____

Will results be affected if larger plates are used?_____

Is the weight of the pennies a greater factor than the size of the plate? _____

As an extension, have students try a variety of Styrofoam plate sizes, or a collection of aluminum foil shapes, on which to place pennies.

- -

Dear Parents/Guardians,

We will be conducting an experiment about sinking and floating which requires aluminum foil or Styrofoam plates in a variety of sizes. Please collect these items and have your child bring them to school by_____. Thank you for your donation to this project.

Sincerely,

_____

Tree Rings

Relate the 100th Day to birthdays, Johnny Appleseed, the study of plants, Earth Day, or Arbor Day with this lesson on determining the age of a tree through a cross section of its rings. Introduce the topic by asking students how they know their ages. Show them a picture or slide of a tree, or a real pine, oak, or evergreen tree and ask for a hypothesis about its age. Explain that a tree's age can be determined by counting its rings, with one ring being added for every year of life. If possible, go outside to an area with trees and let the students act like trees and sway in the breeze.

Materials:

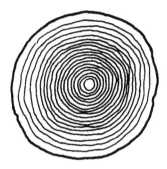

- cross section of a tree, a picture of a cross section, or various sizes of circles
- stencils
- blank paper
- pencils and crayons

Directions:

Take the students outside to study the structure of a tree and then draw and color a picture based on their observations. If there aren't any trees in your area, have the students copy a picture or imagine a tree. Ask them how old their tree is and write that number on the bottom of the tree. Draw a simple diagram of a tree cross section (circles within circles) and demonstrate the counting of the rings to represent the tree's age. Have students use this idea to make circles that reflect the age of the trees in their pictures.

Contact the local 4-H club, state forestry department, or environmental education association and ask if a 100-year-old tree exists in your area. If possible, arrange a trip to see the tree or notify students' families of its existence so that they can go to see it. As a class writing activity, students can write about possible events which took place during the lifetime of the tree, using the tree rings as indicators of weather conditions.

Tree Information: The scientific term for tree dating is *dendrochronology*; the rings are formed annually, and the thickness of each ring reflects the age and environmental conditions such as sunshine, wind, snow, carbon dioxide, and temperature.

Further information may be available from the Laboratory of Tree-Ring Research at the University of Arizona, Tucson.

More Activities:

- Have students draw tree ring cross sections that match their ages, the ages of friends, the ages of family members, etc. Each student can then choose a combination of the tree ring cross sections that total 100 (or more).

- Ask the students to draw a picture of what they think they will look like when they are 100 years old. Follow this with a drawing of a 100-year-old tree.

TV Trees

These attractive trees are made from recycled *TV Guides*. (**Note:** Other magazines of this proportion may be substituted.) The trees can be decorated for Christmas projects, used to create a diorama of 100 trees, used as table decorations, or donated to a local senior citizens' center or pediatric hospital. This project requires more than one class period. It can be an ongoing project that students can work on when they finish their required assignments.

Materials:

- one *TV Guide* per student
- green spray paint or green tempera paint
- paintbrushes
- old newspapers to cover the desk or floor
- assorted pieces of ribbons, buttons, and scraps of fabric or colored paper
- scissors
- tape or glue

Directions:

Distribute one *TV Guide* to each student. Staple or glue the front and back pages together.

Fold each page down to create the tree shape. Demonstrate the folding technique as illustrated below.

Fold each page and then spray or brush paint the tree. Allow one day for it to dry completely.

Decorate the trees with items such as ribbons, bows, buttons, paper birds, and paper nests.

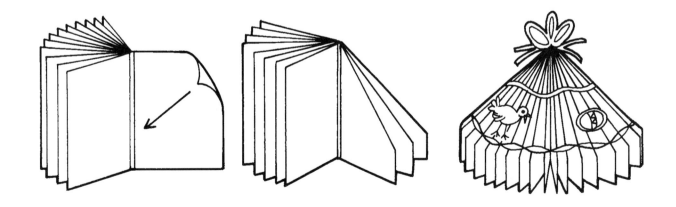

1. Fold upper right corner to inside edge.

2. Glue or staple page in place.

3. Paint, decorate, and enjoy!

Apple Strings

This aromatic apple craft will make a lovely gift or home decoration which your students will enjoy making and be proud to share. The more volunteers you can recruit, the better, because of the cutting involved. The apples can be obtained from the lunch service, as a donation from a local supermarket, or from the students. Remember to ask for the apples a day prior to when you will actually do the project so that anyone who forgets to bring one can still have an opportunity to obtain an apple and participate.

Materials:

- one apple for each student
- paper towels
- shallow bowls
- sharp plastic knives
- lemon juice
- string
- scissors
- (optional: raffia or cloth ribbons)

Directions:

Place the apples on a table and let the students examine the different types. After they wash their hands, have students group the apples in different categories according to color, shape, size, and smell. With the assistance of the parents, carefully slice the apples to make circles. The students may taste the top and bottom sections, or you can save these for apple paint prints. Have the students carefully poke out and collect the seeds. Use these for comparisons and to plant later. Distribute an 18-inch (46 cm) piece of string to each student. Thread each slice through a seed hole and tie the ends to form a circle. Dip the ring of apples into lemon juice and hang to dry in a warm spot over a period of several days. The apple rings should be spaced far enough apart so they can dry thoroughly with good air circulation. They can be hung on door knobs, hooks, or by clothespins. Observe the changes in the slices as they dry. They can be decorated with raffia or cloth ribbons and used as holiday ornaments, natural decorations, or door wreaths.

Nesting Dolls

Your students will enjoy creating these charming nesting dolls as part of your 100th Day celebration. Professionally made nesting dolls are available in many stores, especially during the winter holiday season. The decor has expanded from traditional Russian or Polish women to cartoon and political figures. For primary students, this project can be expanded to learn about sizes: small, medium, large or big, bigger, biggest. Older students can count by multiples of four to reach 100, relating this to multiplication and division facts.

Materials:

- containers: egg cartons, milk cartons, paper cones, plastic cups from ice cream sundaes, small fast-food restaurant cups, plastic drinking cups in assorted sizes, yogurt containers, cottage cheese containers, margarine containers, empty film canisters, etc.
- glue and tape
- markers, crayons, or paint
- assorted odds and ends of ribbons, felt, fabric, buttons, paper scraps

Directions:

Each student will need four containers of different sizes which will comfortably nest inside each other. If possible, display a set of wooden nesting dolls and show the students how they can be opened so that the smaller figures fit inside the larger ones. Choose a decorating theme such as the growth cycle of a plant, sports personalities, inventors, storybook characters, people in history, or family members. Position the containers upside down so that the opening is on the desk. The students use the odds and ends to decorate their three containers according to their theme. When finished, the characters can be used to create a story such as *The Three Little Pigs*, *Goldilocks and the Three Bears*, *My Pets*, or *My Family*. The pupils can construct a puppet theater or stage from a large box or use the tops of their desks. Invite other classes and parents to view your performance.

Animation

Provide your students with the chance to be illustrators of their own animated moving picture with this introduction to animation. You can expand this into a career awareness activity by arranging for illustrators, local artists, or community college art students to be class guests. Because of the amount of drawing involved, this project should be planned over a week-long period. Another option is to begin it during class on a Thursday or Friday and then let the students take it home to do during the weekend. It's a good idea to prepare a model of your own to demonstrate how to illustrate motion.

Materials:

- stapler
- glue
- pencils, crayons
- reproduction paper or unlined 3" x 5" (8 cm x 13 cm) memo pads

Directions:

Divide the class into groups of five students. Each group will produce a flip book of 100 pages, with each student contributing 20 pages. (For class sizes not divisible by five, make group sizes as close as possible to five and adjust pages per student accordingly.)

If you use memo pads, give each child 20 sheets stapled together at one end. If you used reproduction paper, cut the paper in half lengthwise, then fold twice, and cut the paper in four equal sections. This will produce 10 sheets of 4" by 2" (10 cm by 5 cm) paper. Arrange the paper so all of the uncut straight edge of the paper is as even as possible on the flipping side. Staple or glue the other end securely with three or four staples across. Discuss with your students how to choose a subject to draw which shows some noticeable motion. Some possibilities are a fisherman catching a fish, a dog chasing a squirrel up a tree, a horse jumping a fence, a person walking, a child doing a cartwheel, an acrobat on a trapeze, or anything that stirs the imagination.

Start with one student in the group. Have him or her draw the chosen figure on the first page. On the next page, draw the figure with a slight motion, moving the page back and forth to coordinate the motion. The student continues drawing the 20 pages in this way until a segment of motion is completed. The next student in the group creates his or her drawings in the same way, continuing the motion of the previous student's figure. When a group has completed its 100-page flip book, have the members glue their segments together in order. Share the groups' flip books. To set the illustrations in motion, grasp the glued edge and flip the book from the bottom or side. It takes practice to flip smoothly.

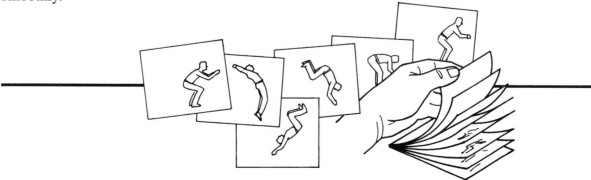

Follow-up and Extension Ideas

◆ Create a class booklet to share with peers and families titled "Our Favorite Things to Do for the 100th Day of School."

◆ Continue counting the number of school days.

◆ Create a stamp celebrating the 100th day of school and submit it to the U.S. Postal Service in Washington, D.C., as a possible future stamp.

◆ On the 101st day, read or watch *101 Dalmatians* and then tell, write, and/or illustrate what will happen next.

◆ Read weather reports from around the world to determine if there is a place where the weather temperature matches the number of that day. For instance, on the 101st day, is there a place where the temperature is 101 degrees?

◆ Have a bowl-a-thon, predicting and observing who can score the same number of points as the number day.

◆ Have a student and family 100th Day Dance.

◆ During April celebrate National TV Turn-off Week by compiling a list of 100 things to do instead of watching TV. Predict and then observe who can last 100 hours without watching TV.

◆ During spring have a school walk-a-thon fund-raiser to raise money for your library, playground equipment, media center, or other worthy cause. As a class, set goals to walk the total of miles that corresponds to that school number day or try to raise that much money.

◆ For Earth Day or Arbor Day, plant 100 seeds or tree sprouts in a local park or on school grounds and then take care of them as they grow.

◆ During June have a class snack of watermelon. Collect and count the seeds to observe if you have more or less than 100.

◆ Compile a list of 100 or more activities you can do during the summer break.

◆ Make a list of 100 books for summertime reading, including your personal favorites. Borrow them from the library or purchase the books from a bookstore for summer reading pleasure.

Follow-up and Extension Ideas (cont.)

✦ Use a computer, read books, or take a trip to a natural history museum to learn about animals, including people, that have more than 100 bones; construct models of the skeletons.

✦ In anticipation of Flag Day in June, study about the hundreds of flags of different states and countries. Design and create a school flag and obtain approval to have it displayed.

✦ During March have students in the upper grades make 100 shamrocks and pieces of gold and hide them throughout the school grounds. Have the older students team with younger students to find the hidden shamrocks. Can they find all 100?

✦ Use decks of cards to create houses. Can you use 100 cards with which to build and still keep your house standing up?

✦ Participate in the Jump Rope for Heart event sponsored by the American Heart Association. Predict and actually count the number of jumps a person makes in two minutes and how much money, in multiples of 100, is raised for the Association.

✦ For Earth Day and Arbor Day, make a list of 100 or more things we can do to improve our environment. Choose several for class projects.

✦ Have a letter-writing campaign to send postcards and letters to 100 people in the armed services overseas.

✦ On or before the 100th day of school, have the students bring in a plain white or pale colored T-shirt. Have the students autograph each other's shirts with permanent markers or paint. Try to get 100 autographs on each shirt. Have students wear their shirts on the 100th day.

✦ Just before the end of the school year, create a booklet in which students and their families can describe and illustrate the events of their summer. Title the booklet "100 Summer Things I Did."

✦ Have a teach-a-thon. Think of something you and your students can do such as whistle, sing a special song, tie your shoes, or play hand-clapping games such as Miss Mary Mack. Teach this to other students and family members. Graph and tally how many people you have taught. Have you taught 101, 201 . . .?